MARTIN LUTHER KING JR.

CIVIL RIGHTS LEADER

"I have a dream
that one day this nation will rise up
and live out the true meaning of its creed:
'We hold this to be self-evident,
that all men are created equal.'"
~ Martin Luther King Jr. ~

BY ANDREW SANTELLA

Published by The Child's World®
1980 Lookout Drive • Mankato, MN 56003-1705
800-599-READ • www.childsworld.com

CONTENT CONSULTANT
Susan Englander, PhD, Assistant Editor,
Martin Luther King, Jr. Papers Project at Stanford University

PHOTOS
Cover and page 4: AP Photo
Interior: alisafarov/Shutterstock.com: 8; AP Photo: 5, 7, 12, 15, 19, 20, 22, 24, 26, 29,
31; AP Photo/Gene Herrick: 17, 18; AP Photo/JAB: 6; AP Photo/James A. Mills: 14; AP
Photo/The Herald, File: 21; Courtesy Barack Obama Presidential Library: 27; Don
Rice/Library of Congress, Prints and Photographs Division: 25; Everett Collection/
Shutterstock.com: 10; © Flip Schulke/CORBIS/Corbis via Getty Images: 13; Jack
Delano/Library of Congress, Prints and Photographs Division: 11; JT Vintage/
ZUMA Press/Newscom: 23; Keystone View Company/Library of Congress, Prints
and Photographs Division: 9; Michael Ochs Archives via Getty Images: 16, 28

LIBRARY OF CONGRESS CATALOGING-IN-PUBLICATION DATA
ISBN 9781503854475 (Reinforced Library Binding)
ISBN 9781503854925 (Portable Document Format)
ISBN 9781503855304 (Online Multi-user eBook)
LCCN: 2021930455

Printed in the United States of America

Cover and page 4 caption:
Dr. Martin Luther King in 1963.

CONTENTS

Chapter One

THE MARCH ON WASHINGTON

On a steamy August day in 1963, a vast crowd gathered in
front of the Lincoln Memorial in Washington, DC. There were
enough people in this one area of the nation's capitol to fill a
medium-sized city. In all, about 250,000 people had made their
way to the monument. They included poor farmers and college
professors, ministers and movie stars. People of all backgrounds
had come to Washington from every part of the country. They
were there to demand freedom and justice for African Americans.
They called their gathering the March on Washington for Jobs
and Freedom.

Thousands of marchers
gather at the Lincoln
Memorial and its reflecting
pool for the March on
Washington for Jobs
and Freedom in 1963.

In many places in the United States in 1963, African Americans were not free to live where they liked. They could not send their children to the best public schools. Unfair laws denied some Black citizens the right to vote.

Martin Luther King Jr. chats with a Mississippi family about the importance of voting.

The people gathered for the March on Washington for Jobs and Freedom were determined to end such injustice. For leadership, they looked to one man above all others. He was not a powerful politician, or a general, or the head of a huge company. He was a **pastor** at a Baptist church in Atlanta, Georgia. His name was Martin Luther King Jr.

For eight years, King had been leading the struggle to win basic rights for African Americans. He had led marches and protests. He had endured violent abuse. Several times, he had been arrested and thrown in jail for demanding his rights as an American citizen. His work had made him famous all over the world.

Still, King had never spoken to a crowd as large as the one gathered on August 28, 1963. People filled every inch of space on the lawn in front of the Lincoln Memorial. Thousands more around the world watched on television.

On the speaker's platform, King began reading a speech he had written for the occasion. About halfway through his speech, he stopped reading and started speaking from his heart. He told the crowd about a dream he had. "I have a dream," he said, "that my four little children will one day live in a nation where they will not be judged by the color of their skin, but by the content of their character."

As King spoke, people in the crowd shouted out their support. Some people joined hands and swayed back and forth. King went on, "I have a dream that one day…little Black boys and Black girls will be able to join hands with little white boys and white girls as sisters and brothers."

"And when this happens," King continued, "we will be able…to join hands and sing in the words of the old Negro spiritual, 'Free at last! Free at last! Thank God almighty, we are free at last!'"

King did not live to see his dream come true. But his dream would live on in the hearts of the many Americans he inspired.

After delivering his speech at the Lincoln Memorial, King and other civil rights leaders met with President Kennedy and Vice President Johnson at the White House to discuss the civil rights movement. A year later, the landmark Civil Rights Act of 1964 was passed, which made it illegal to discriminate against people based on race, sex, or religion. Congress then passed the Voting Rights Act of 1965, which allowed the government to overturn laws in states that made voting harder for Black people and other minorities.

Martin Luther King Jr. addresses thousands of civil rights supporters in front of the Lincoln Memorial on August 28, 1963.

Chapter Two

THE PASTOR'S SON

Martin Luther King Jr. was born Michael King Jr. in Atlanta on
January 15, 1929. About five years later, both he and his father
changed their names to Martin Luther King (around the house,
Martin Jr. was simply called M. L.). Martin Luther was an
important religious leader of the 1500s, and religion was an
important part of the King household.

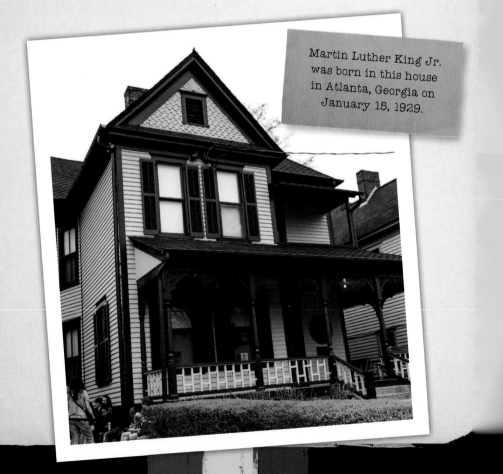

Martin Luther King Jr.
was born in this house
in Atlanta, Georgia on
January 15, 1929.

Atlanta, Georgia in 1929.

M. L.'s father was the pastor of Ebenezer Baptist Church. M. L.'s grandfather on his mother's side had been pastor of the church before him. On Sundays, the entire King family spent all day at church. M. L., his sister Willie Christine, and his brother Alfred Daniel attended services and Bible study. Their mother, Alberta Williams King, played the church organ.

In many ways, M. L. had a typical childhood. He delivered newspapers to earn spending money and spent his free time flying kites and model airplanes. He loved sports, too, and especially enjoyed rough-and-tumble games of football on empty lots in his neighborhood. Even before he started school, he displayed an eagerness to read as much as he could.

But all was not well in M. L.'s world. He was growing up Black in a nation controlled by powerful white people. This meant that M. L. could not enjoy the same rights and **privileges** as white people.

Martin Luther King Jr.'s childhood home and the Ebenezer Baptist Church in Atlanta, Georgia, are National Historic Sites. Visitors can tour King's birthplace and make the short walk to the church. King's funeral service was also held at Ebenezer Baptist in April 1968. Thousands of people showed up and listened to the service broadcasted outside over loudspeakers.

A segregated movie theater in Mississippi in 1939.

In the South, whites and African Americans attended separate schools and churches. In public places, African Americans had to drink from water fountains marked "colored." They used separate "colored" bathrooms in train stations and at bus depots. They swam in "colored" swimming pools if there were any available. In most aspects of everyday life, African Americans were kept separate—or segregated—from whites. On election day, African Americans were too often denied the voting rights that whites enjoyed. In some places, for example, Black citizens were unfairly required to pass reading tests or to pay fees before voting.

At a young age, M. L. learned about the unfairness of **segregation**. In preschool, one of his playmates was a white boy. When the time came for the two boys to start elementary school, they had to enroll in separate schools. What's more, the white boy's parents decided that their son should no longer play with M. L. The reason was simple. Their son was white. And M. L. was Black.

Unsurprisingly, this decision hurt and disturbed young M. L. His mother gave him some advice that stayed with him for the rest of his life. M. L.'s father later remembered his wife's words as "Never think, son, that there is anything that makes a person better than you are, especially the color of his skin."

A classroom of Black students in Georgia in 1941.

Chapter Three

THE EDUCATION
OF A LEADER

Young M. L. grew up quickly. At six years old, he was singing church hymns with his mother in front of audiences. At 13, he entered Booker T. Washington High School in Atlanta. When he was just 15 years old, he passed the college entrance exams that allowed him to enroll at Morehouse College in Atlanta.

Morehouse had started a special program that allowed gifted younger students to begin college early. High school–age students like M. L. could take the place of college students who had gone off to fight in World War II. Morehouse was a natural choice for M. L. Both his father and his mother's father had attended the school. M. L. lived at home while he attended college, and he concentrated on his studies. He received good grades, especially in English and social science.

King, in dark jacket, listens to a lecture at Morehouse College.

Martin Luther King Jr. lived in this dormitory as he studied for his degree from Crozer Theological Seminary.

As he neared graduation, M. L. tried to decide on a career path. He was interested in medicine and in law, but eventually decided on another profession: his father's. He would become a minister. No one was more pleased with the decision than Martin Sr. In February 1948, M. L. was **ordained** a Baptist minister, and he graduated from Morehouse that spring.

The young minister left Atlanta in 1948, having decided to work toward a bachelor of divinity degree at Crozer Theological **Seminary** in Chester, Pennsylvania. This experience was his first chance to attend a school with both white and African American students. King involved himself deeply in campus life, and he served as president of the senior class.

King was only 19 years old when Gandhi died in 1948, so the two leaders never met. In 1959, Martin and his wife, Coretta, traveled to Gandhi's homeland to meet the people of India and give talks. King later wrote that "I left India more convinced than ever before that non-violent resistance is the most potent weapon available to oppressed people in their struggle for freedom."

It may have been at Crozer that King first learned about the ideas of Indian leader Mohandas Gandhi. Using marches, strikes, and other peaceful methods, Gandhi had led the struggle for India's independence from Great Britain. King was fascinated by Gandhi's **philosophy**, and he read everything he could about his life and work. Gandhi's ideas and accomplishments later served as the model for King's work in the United States.

King finished his studies at Crozer at the top of his class. He was chosen to give a speech at his graduation and won a **scholarship** to pay for further study. He used the money to enroll in Boston University's School of Theology, where he began working toward a doctorate—the most advanced degree in higher education.

Mohandas Gandhi was a famous Indian leader whose peaceful beliefs greatly influenced King. Gandhi was shot and killed on January 30, 1948.

The King family in March 1963. Their fourth child was born a few days after this photo was taken.

In Boston, he also met a music student named Coretta Scott. She was studying at a nearby music school, and the two began dating. They quickly fell in love. The couple married on June 18, 1953, at the Scott family home in Alabama.

In the meantime, King knew exactly what he wanted to do after he finished his studies in Boston. He had decided to return to the South, where he would serve as the pastor of a church.

Chapter Four

MONTGOMERY

In 1954, Martin Luther King Jr. became pastor of Dexter Avenue Baptist Church in Montgomery, Alabama. King jumped into his new job with great energy and passion. He impressed the members of his church with his fiery sermons and his concern for the needy. He encouraged them to vote and to take part in the political life of their community. He urged them to join the National Association for the Advancement of Colored People (NAACP), which was the nation's leading **civil rights group**.

Reverend Martin Luther King Jr. became pastor of Dexter Avenue Baptist Church in Montgomery in 1954.

Rosa Parks getting
fingerprinted following
her arrest.

At the same time, King was completing his schooling. In 1955, he was awarded his doctorate from Boston University. The same year, Coretta gave birth to a daughter named Yolanda Denise. Then came an event that changed King's life and the lives of many Americans.

On December 1, 1955, an African American woman named Rosa Parks stepped on board a Montgomery bus on her way home from work. Parks refused to give up her seat to a white passenger. In Montgomery, a law required that African Americans give up their seats to whites if the buses were full. Parks was arrested and thrown in jail.

A crowd of supporters cheer for King, who had just been found guilty of leading the Montgomery bus boycott in March 1956.

Parks's arrest outraged African Americans in Montgomery. Some decided to organize a **boycott** of the Montgomery buses, and they chose King as their leader. They hoped that by refusing to ride the buses, they would pressure the city into improving the way it treated African Americans.

King kept busy by speaking and encouraging car pools for Black citizens to get around. "We have no alternative but to protest," King told supporters in Montgomery. However, he insisted that the protest be a peaceful one. We must meet the forces of hate with the power of love," he said, repeating Gandhi's words.

The forces of hate were not easily defeated. On January 30, 1956, someone placed a bomb on the front porch of King's home. It exploded and broke the windows of the house, but no one was hurt.

By threatening King's family, somebody was trying to frighten King into giving up his protest. It didn't work. The

Two Black men sit at the front of a bus in Montgomery after the Supreme Court's ruling in December 1956.

boycott went on for more than a year, and finally justice won out. On November 13, 1956, the U.S. Supreme Court made segregation on buses in Alabama illegal. Never again was it legal for a Montgomery bus driver to ask Black passengers to give up their seats to white people.

Chapter Five

A NATIONAL LEADER

The victory in Montgomery helped make King famous across the country. He formed a group called the Southern Christian Leadership Conference (SCLC) to lead the drive for civil rights in the South. His picture appeared on the cover of national magazines. He was invited to speak at colleges and churches all over the United States.

However, King's fame also exposed him to new dangers. On a visit to New York in 1958, he was attacked and stabbed by a disturbed woman. King recovered from the wound, but for the rest of his life he had to live with the threat of violence against him and his family.

Martin Luther King Jr. speaks in Atlanta in 1960.

In 1959, the Kings traveled to India, the land where Gandhi had used nonviolent protest to win his people's freedom. In India, King met with Gandhi's followers and was inspired by their determination to end injustice.

At the same time, more people in the United States were turning to nonviolent protest. In 1960, groups of students in several southern states challenged whites-only laws at lunch counters. Their protests were called **sit-ins** because the protesters refused to move from the lunch counter until they were served. The sit-ins forced more than 100 southern cities in the United States to end segregation at lunch counters.

In 1960, King moved back to Atlanta and accepted his father's offer to become co-pastor at Ebenezer Baptist Church. He continued to support sit-ins and other forms of peaceful protest. But African Americans in the South still had to live with segregation and **discrimination**.

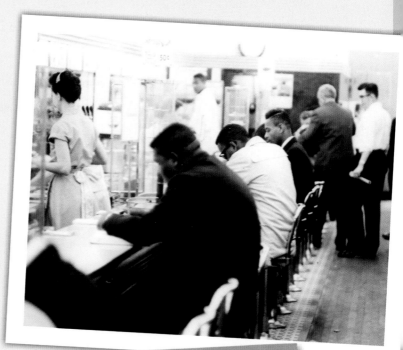

Young men participate in a lunch counter sit-in in South Carolina in 1960.

One of the toughest places to be an African American was Birmingham, Alabama. Public facilities there were segregated, and local merchants rarely hired Black workers. The city's commissioner of public safety, T. Eugene "Bull" Connor, and his police treated African Americans brutally.

In 1963, King and the SCLC set their sights on Birmingham. "We felt if we could crack that city, we could crack any city," he said later.

King was arrested for leading a march demanding an end to segregation in Birmingham. While he sat in his Birmingham jail cell, he wrote a letter explaining the principles of nonviolent protest. "There are two types of laws: just and unjust," King wrote. "I would be the first to advocate obeying just laws…[but] one has a moral responsibility to disobey unjust laws." King's "Letter from Birmingham Jail" was quickly published as a pamphlet, and more than one million people read it.

Meanwhile, the protests in Birmingham continued, and even high school and grade school children joined in. Police turned high-pressure water hoses on young demonstrators and allowed attack dogs to bite some of them. Images of the police tactics appeared on national television and in newspapers, shocking the nation. Upon his release from jail, King asserted that the eyes of the world were watching Birmingham.

An officer leads King to a police vehicle as King heads to the Birmingham jail on April 13, 1963.

The events in Birmingham helped push the nation's leaders into action. That year, President John F. Kennedy proposed legislation outlawing segregation in public facilities.

To rally support for the proposed law, King organized the peaceful March on Washington for Jobs and Freedom on August 28, 1963. Before those 250,000 people who were gathered at the Lincoln Memorial, King delivered his historic "I Have a Dream" speech. He said his goal was "to arouse the conscience of the nation." He succeeded.

Congress soon passed the Civil Rights Act of 1964, which outlawed discrimination in the workplace, schools, and in public places. For his part in making the law a reality and for his practice of nonviolent protest, King was awarded the Nobel Peace Prize later that year. The prestigious prize honors the person who does the best work to promote international peace during the previous year. At 35, King was the youngest person ever to receive a Nobel Prize.

In his "Letter from Birmingh[am]" King explained why it was n[ecessary] to take action, even if it me[ant] breaking the law and being [arrested]. He believed that creating "[tension and] pressure" was the only way [to] get people's attention and e[ffect] positive change. "Injustice [anywhere] is a threat to justice everyw[here]," King wrote. "Whatever affe[cts one] directly, affects all indirectl[y]."

King holding his Nobel Peace Prize medal on December 10, 1964.

Chapter Six

THE FINAL YEARS

The Civil Rights Act was a great step forward for racial equality. King knew, however, that there was still more work to do. One of his goals was to increase the number of African American voters. In many places, unfair laws still kept some African Americans from voting in elections.

In Selma, Alabama, only a few hundred of the city's 15,000 African American residents were registered to vote. In 1965, King led hundreds of African Americans in marches to the Selma courthouse, where they tried to register to vote. On February 1, 1965, King was arrested for violating the city's laws governing parades. He was released from jail after five days.

The Kings leading the march from Selma to Montgomery in 1965.

King speaking in 1967.

In March, a group of protesters tried to march from Selma to the state capital of Montgomery. Along the way, the march was brutally broken up by state troopers swinging clubs. Several weeks later, King was finally able to lead marchers to Montgomery. The protests helped win support for the Voting Rights Act of 1965. This act made it illegal to discriminate against voters of any race. It also made it illegal to intimidate voters and outlawed practices that kept any American from voting.

Of course, racial injustice was not just a southern problem. In northern cities, African Americans often lived in poor, all-Black neighborhoods. In 1966, King went to Chicago to protest segregation in housing. He led marches in all-white neighborhoods, where African Americans were never allowed to live. However, his protests there had little effect.

At the same time, a new generation of African American leaders was questioning King's peaceful approach. New leaders such as Stokely Carmichael used the slogan "Black Power" and encouraged African Americans to fight back against injustice.

King continued to preach nonviolence. In 1967, he spoke out against involvement in the Vietnam War. More and more, he focused on ending poverty and unemployment, not just among African Americans but in all communities. He began to lay plans for a massive but peaceful Poor People's March on Washington. However, his plans were interrupted by a call from Memphis, Tennessee.

Coretta Scott King was not just the wife of the leader of the civil rights movement. She was an effective activist in her own right. After Martin Luther King's death, Coretta continued the work, speaking out about racism and marching against injustice in the United States and abroad. She became a best-selling author and established the King Center, which aims to teach Dr. King's message and inspire future generations to continue to fight for equality.

Sanitation workers in Memphis were on strike to win fair wages and better working conditions. King went to Memphis to speak to the striking workers and to support them. In a speech on April 3, 1968, he urged his audience to keep working for justice and equality. "I've seen the promised land!" he declared. "I may not get there with you, but I want you to know tonight that we as a people will get to the promised land."

The next day, King was relaxing on the balcony outside his Memphis motel room. Suddenly and horribly, a gunshot rang out from a building across the street. King fell, wounded in the head and neck. He was pronounced dead at a nearby hospital within an hour. He was just 39 years old.

Coretta Scott King sits in front of Martin Luther King Jr.'s casket on April 9, 1968.

Nearly one year later, a drifter named James Earl Ray pleaded guilty to firing the shot that killed King. He was sentenced to 99 years in prison.

From the mid-1950s until his death in 1968, Martin Luther King Jr. was one of the principal leaders of the movement for civil rights. Even though his life was cut short, his achievements were remarkable. He helped end the legal system of segregation that had made African Americans second-class citizens. His peaceful protests called attention to injustice and **racism**. His stirring words rallied African Americans to demand their basic rights as Americans. Those words continue to inspire people of all backgrounds.

President Barack Obama, America's first Black president, toured the Martin Luther King Jr. National Memorial in Washington, DC in 2011.

King was buried at Southview Cemetery in Atlanta on April 9, 1968. Two years later, his body was moved to the Martin Luther King, Jr. Center for Nonviolent Social Change (also called the "King Center"). Carved into the stone of his burial place are the words he had spoken at the Lincoln Memorial in 1963:

"Free at last, Free at last,

Thank God Almighty

I'm Free at last."

What are the ideas and philosophies that drove King's work?
Do some research and compare and contrast
King's work with that of Mohandas Gandhi.

**What are the strengths and weaknesses
of peaceful protesting?**
Explain your answer.

TIME LINE

1920-1940

1929
Martin Luther King Jr. is born on January 15 in Atlanta, Georgia.

1944
At the age of 15, King begins studying at Morehouse College in Atlanta.

1948
King is ordained a Baptist minister. He graduates from Morehouse College and goes on to Crozer Theological Seminary.

1950

1953
King marries Coretta Scott on June 18.

1954
King becomes pastor of Dexter Avenue Baptist Church in Montgomery, Alabama.

1955
King is awarded a doctorate in theology from Boston University. He leads a boycott of the Montgomery, Alabama, bus system, after Rosa Parks refuses to give up her seat to a white passenger.

1956
King's home is bombed. The Montgomery boycott continues. On November 13, the U.S. Supreme Court rules segregation on buses in Alabama is illegal.

1957
King forms a group called the Southern Christian Leadership Conference (SCLC) to lead the drive for civil rights in the South.

1958
King is attacked and stabbed by a disturbed woman on a visit to New York.

1959
The Kings travel to India, where Gandhi had used nonviolent protest to win his people's freedom.

**King fought to end segregation in his lifetime,
yet Black people still face injustice daily.**
What are examples of racism today?

**If you could write three new laws that every person
had to follow, what would they be and why?**
Explain your answer.

1960
King moves back to Atlanta to become co-pastor at Ebenezer Baptist Church with his father.

1963
On August 28, some 250,000 people gather for the March on Washington for Jobs and Freedom. King gives his historic "I Have a Dream" speech at the Lincoln Memorial.

1964
King wins the Nobel Peace Prize. The U.S. Congress passes the Civil Rights Act.

1965
King leads a voting rights campaign in Selma, Alabama. Congress passes the Voting Rights Act.

1966
King goes to Chicago to protest segregation in housing.

1968
King is shot and killed in Memphis, Tennessee, on April 4. He is buried at Southview Cemetery in Atlanta on April 9.

1970
King's body is moved to the Martin Luther King, Jr. Center for Nonviolent Social Change.

1977
Nine years after his death, King is awarded the Presidential Medal of Freedom.

2016
The U.S. Treasury announces that King will be featured on the back of the $5 bill.

boycott (BOY-kot)
A boycott is the act of refusing to buy or use a product or service as a protest. In 1955, King led a boycott of the Montgomery bus system.

**civil rights group
(SIV-il RITES GROOP)**
A civil rights group is an organization that works to gain equal laws and equal rights for all citizens. The National Association for the Advancement of Colored People (NAACP) is one of the nation's leading civil rights groups.

**discrimination
(diss-KRIM-uh-NAY-shun)**
Discrimination is the act of treating people unfairly based on their race, sex, or background. African Americans faced legal discrimination for many years in the United States.

ordained (or-DAYND)
To be ordained means to be officially appointed a minister. King was ordained a Baptist minister in 1947.

pastor (PASS-tur)
A pastor is a minister of a church. King and his father were both pastors.

philosophy (fuh-LOSS-uh-fee)
A philosophy is a person's basic ideas and beliefs about how to live. Indian leader Mohandas Gandhi's philosophies, which were rooted in peaceful protest, greatly influenced King.

privileges (PRIV-uh-lid-jiz)
Privileges are special rights or advantages. Growing up in the South, King did not have the same rights and privileges as white citizens.

racism (RAY-siz-um)
Racism is the belief that one race of people is better than another. African Americans often faced racism throughout the history of the United States.

scholarship (SKAHL-ur-ship)
A scholarship is a grant or a prize that pays for college. After graduating from Crozer Theological Seminary, King won a scholarship for further study.

segregation (seg-ruh-GAY-shuhn)
Segregation is the practice of keeping racial groups apart. Segregation is no longer legal in the United States.

seminary (SEM-uh-nayr-ee)
A seminary is a school that trains ministers, priests, or rabbis. King earned a bachelor of divinity degree at Crozer Theological Seminary in Pennsylvania.

sit-ins (SIT-ins)
Sit-ins are a form of protest in which people enter a public place and refuse to leave for a long period of time. In 1960, students staged sit-ins to protest segregation at lunch counters.

BOOKS

Bader, Bonnie. *Who Was Martin Luther King, Jr.?* New York, NY: Grosset & Dunlap, 2016.

Clark-Robinson, Monica. *Let the Children March*. Solon, OH: Findaway World, 2019.

Harrison, Vashti. *Little Legends: Exceptional Men in Black History*. New York, NY: Little, Brown and Company, 2019.

Platt, Christine. *Trailblazers: Martin Luther King, Jr.: Fighting for Civil Rights*. New York, NY: Random House Children's Books, 2020.

Venable, Rose. *The Civil Rights Movement*. Mankato, MN: The Child's World, 2021.

WEBSITES

Visit our website for links about Martin Luther King Jr.:

childsworld.com/links

Note to Parents, Teachers, and Librarians: We routinely verify our Web links to make sure they are safe, active sites—so encourage your readers to check them out!

INDEX